COMPANY CULTURE IN ARTS ORGANIZATIONS

RESISTANCE TO MODERNIZING INFRASTRUCTURE AND
THE ROLE OF CULTURAL OPERATIONS SPECIALISTS

DENISE ZUBIZARRETA

© Denise Zubizarreta

Denise Zubizarreta
LEAP Institute for the Arts
Arts Leadership & Cultural Management
Colorado State University

For Tya.

TABLE OF CONTENTS

Prologue — 8

Chapter 1 — 9

The Resistance to Modernizing Infrastructure — 9

Financial Constraints and Resource Allocation — 9

Lack of Understanding of Modern Management Practices — 10

Psychological Barriers and Aversion to Change — 11

Organizational Inertia and the "Crisis of Leadership" — 12

The Impact of Resistance on Organizational Performance — 12

The Consequences of Stagnation: A Case for Modernization — 13

Toward a Culture of Adaptation and Modernization — 14

Chapter 2 — 15

The Executive Director Conundrum — 15

The Burden of Being a "Jack of All Trades" — 15

The Impact of Antiquated Infrastructure on Delegation — 16

The Vicious Cycle of Overwhelm and Organizational Stagnation — 17

The Psychological Toll of Role Overload	18
The Hidden Costs of the Executive Director Conundrum	19
The Need for Structural Change and Support	20

Chapter 3   22

Structural Problems and Their Impact on Staff   22

Lack of Guidance and Autonomy	22
Disempowerment and Reduced Job Satisfaction	23
High Turnover and Loss of Institutional Knowledge	24
Compounded by Lack of Investment in Professional Development	24
Stagnation and Reduced Organizational Capacity	25
The Importance of Addressing Structural Problems	26

Chapter 4   28

The Role of Cultural Operations Specialists   28

Defining the Cultural Operations Specialist	28
Expertise in Organizational Development and Change Management	29
Strategic Planning and Mission Alignment	30
Building a Positive and Productive Company Culture	31
Modernizing Infrastructure to Support Organizational Goals	32

Driving Innovation and Adaptability   33

Navigating Financial Sustainability and Community Engagement   33

The Catalyst for Sustainable Growth   34

Chapter 5   36

Reinvigorating Company Culture   36

Understanding the Importance of Company Culture in Arts Organizations   36

Rediscovering and Embracing Core Values   37

Integrating Values into Every Aspect of Operations   38

Building a Culture of Trust and Collaboration   39

Promoting Recognition and Celebrating Successes   40

Addressing Cultural Gaps and Challenges   41

Measuring Impact and Continuous Improvement   42

Chapter 6   43

Practical Strategies for Modernizing Infrastructure   43

A Phased Approach to Modernization   43

Conducting a Thorough Audit of Existing Processes   44

Prioritizing Areas for Targeted Investment   45

Investing in Training and Professional Development   46

Creating Inclusive Feedback Mechanisms   47

Leveraging Technology for Accessibility and Inclusivity 48

Building a Culture of Continuous Improvement   49

Chapter 7   51

The Benefits of a Modernized and Culturally Aligned Organization   51

Greater Efficiency and Resource Optimization   51

Strengthening Company Culture and Enhancing Employee Engagement   52

Enhancing Artistic and Community Impact   53

Building Resilience in an Ever-Changing Landscape   54

Supporting Leadership and Improving Decision-Making   54

Fostering Inclusivity and Accessibility   55

Attracting and Retaining Talent and Support   56

About the Author   58

PROLOGUE

Company culture is a critical component of any organization's success, but in arts organizations, its importance becomes even more pronounced. As entities that exist at the intersection of creativity and administration, arts organizations face unique challenges in balancing artistic vision with operational needs. In recent years, a resistance to modernizing infrastructure has emerged as a critical issue in many arts organizations, leading to a concentration of responsibilities at the executive director (ED) level and a breakdown in the delegation of tasks across staff members.

This imbalance often creates structural issues, impacting both the organization's mission and its staff's morale and efficiency. In response, the role of cultural operations specialists has become increasingly pivotal in restructuring these environments and ensuring that arts organizations remain mission-driven by fostering a healthy and dynamic company culture.

CHAPTER 1

THE RESISTANCE TO MODERNIZING INFRASTRUCTURE

Arts organizations, by their nature, often embody a sense of tradition, nostalgia, and continuity with the past. This is evident in their reverence for classical art forms, historical narratives, and cultural heritage. While this commitment to preserving and celebrating the past is integral to the mission of many arts organizations, it can also foster a mindset that resists change, particularly when it comes to modernizing operational infrastructure. This resistance is frequently rooted in multiple interconnected factors, ranging from financial constraints to psychological barriers, and it can have profound implications for the organization's effectiveness and sustainability.

Financial Constraints and Resource Allocation

One of the most significant barriers to modernization is financial. Many arts organizations operate with limited budgets, often relying heavily on grants, donations, and ticket sales to fund their operations. These financial limitations make it challenging to allocate resources toward modernizing infrastructure, which may be perceived as a secondary priority compared to immediate programmatic needs or artistic production. Investing in new technologies, whether it be digital asset management systems, customer relationship management (CRM) software, or updated accounting platforms, often requires a substantial upfront cost and a commitment to ongoing expenses for maintenance and training. In an environment where every dollar is scrutinized, these costs can seem prohibitive.

Additionally, funding bodies, donors, and boards of directors may not always prioritize or understand the need for infrastructure improvements. The value of such investments is not as immediately visible or as easily quantifiable as the impact of a new production, exhibition, or community outreach program. Consequently, there is often a reluctance to divert funds from these highly visible initiatives to behind-the-scenes improvements, even if those improvements could ultimately enhance the organization's overall efficiency and capacity for future growth.

Lack of Understanding of Modern Management Practices

Another factor contributing to the resistance to modernization is a lack of understanding of modern management practices within many arts organizations. Leadership, especially in small to mid-sized arts organizations, is often composed of individuals who have risen through the ranks due to their artistic or curatorial expertise rather than their managerial skills. While these leaders may possess deep knowledge and passion for their art form, they may lack experience or training in contemporary management techniques, such as data-driven decision-making, digital marketing, or agile project management.

This gap in knowledge can lead to a fear or mistrust of new technologies and methodologies. Without a clear understanding of the benefits of these tools, leaders may perceive them as complex, unnecessary, or even a threat to the organization's established ways of working. The result is a preference for familiar, albeit outdated, practices and systems that feel safe and manageable. This mindset can be further reinforced by a culture of complacency, where the perceived risk of implementing new technologies outweighs the potential benefits.

Psychological Barriers and Aversion to Change

Resistance to modernization in arts organizations is also influenced by psychological factors, including an aversion to change. Change can be intimidating, especially in environments that are already dealing with significant external pressures, such as fluctuating funding levels, shifting audience demographics, and the ongoing impact of global events like the COVID-19 pandemic. For many in the arts sector, there is a genuine fear that change, particularly in terms of operational processes, could disrupt the delicate balance between artistic integrity and financial viability.

This aversion to change is often rooted in a deeply ingrained belief that "the way things have always been done" is inherently the best or only way to do them. In organizations where staff turnover is low and institutional memory is strong, there may be a strong attachment to legacy practices and a corresponding skepticism toward new approaches. Additionally, there can be a fear that modernizing infrastructure will somehow dilute the organization's mission or values, particularly if those values are closely tied to traditional methods or ways of working.

Organizational Inertia and the "Crisis of Leadership"

Organizational inertia plays a significant role in resisting modernization efforts. Over time, many arts organizations develop entrenched patterns of behavior and decision-making that become difficult to disrupt. This inertia is often exacerbated by a "crisis of leadership," where executive directors and senior managers are so overwhelmed by day-to-day responsibilities that they lack the time, energy, or strategic foresight needed to champion and implement change.

The "crisis of leadership" arises when executive directors, who are already stretched thin by multiple roles—acting as fundraisers, marketers, human resources managers, and community liaisons—are unable to focus on long-term strategic planning. Their energy is consumed by immediate, operational concerns, leaving little room to envision or execute the systemic changes necessary to modernize infrastructure. Without strong leadership advocating for and guiding modernization, it becomes even easier for the organization to continue operating on autopilot, maintaining the status quo.

The Impact of Resistance on Organizational Performance

The cumulative effect of these factors is that many arts organizations find themselves stuck in a cycle of inefficiency and underperformance. The reliance on outdated systems and processes often results in wasted time and resources. For example, using paper-based filing systems or manually updating spreadsheets for donor management can be time-consuming, prone to errors, and lack scalability. Similarly, an over-reliance on email for internal communication can lead to miscommunications, overlooked messages, and a lack of coordinated effort.

These inefficiencies hinder the organization's ability to respond quickly and effectively to new opportunities or challenges. Moreover, the reluctance to adopt modern tools for data analysis and project management limits the organization's capacity to measure its impact, make informed decisions, and engage with stakeholders in a meaningful way. As the cultural and economic landscape continues to evolve rapidly, this resistance to change becomes an existential threat, undermining the organization's relevance, sustainability, and ability to fulfill its mission.

The Consequences of Stagnation: A Case for Modernization

Resistance to modernization not only hampers operational efficiency but also stifles innovation. Arts organizations that remain bound to outdated methods may find it challenging to attract new audiences or engage with younger, more tech-savvy demographics. In an era where digital engagement is becoming increasingly important, organizations that fail to modernize risk being left behind. The inability to adapt to new technologies and ways of working can also make it difficult to form partnerships with other organizations or stakeholders who expect a certain level of technological competence and innovation.

In addition, stagnation can affect staff morale and retention. Employees, particularly younger professionals, may feel frustrated by an organization's resistance to adopting more efficient or innovative tools. They may perceive this resistance as a lack of forward-thinking leadership or a sign that the organization is not committed to growth and development. This can lead to higher turnover rates and difficulty attracting top talent, further exacerbating the organization's challenges.

Toward a Culture of Adaptation and Modernization

To overcome these barriers, arts organizations need to cultivate a culture that embraces change and innovation as essential components of their mission. This does not mean abandoning the values and traditions that define the organization, but rather finding ways to integrate new tools and practices that enhance and support those values. This shift requires a concerted effort from leadership, staff, and stakeholders to recognize the value of modernization and to work collaboratively toward its implementation.

By understanding and addressing the underlying reasons for resistance, arts organizations can begin to make the necessary changes to modernize their infrastructure, improve operational efficiency, and better position themselves for a sustainable and impactful future. It is within this context that cultural operations specialists become vital, providing the expertise and strategic insight needed to navigate these complexities and drive meaningful change.

CHAPTER 2

THE EXECUTIVE DIRECTOR CONUNDRUM

The role of the executive director (ED) in an arts organization is uniquely challenging. Often positioned as the organization's public face and primary leader, the ED is responsible for ensuring that both the artistic vision and operational needs are met. However, in many organizations—especially small to mid-sized ones—the ED's role becomes increasingly complex and burdensome due to an antiquated infrastructure and a lack of modern management practices. This situation creates a host of problems that undermine not only the effectiveness of the ED but also the overall health and mission of the organization.

The Burden of Being a "Jack of All Trades"

In theory, the executive director is meant to focus on high-level strategic planning, vision setting, and stakeholder engagement. However, in practice, EDs often find themselves entangled in a wide range of administrative duties that pull them away from these core responsibilities. This "jack of all trades" approach is particularly common in smaller arts organizations, where limited resources mean that the ED must wear multiple hats to keep the organization running.

The duties that fall to the ED in such situations are vast and varied: from day-to-day financial management, including budgeting, accounting, and payroll, to human resources tasks like hiring, staff evaluations, and conflict resolution. Additionally, the ED may be involved in marketing and communications, overseeing everything from social media strategy to press relations. Fundraising, a critical function for any nonprofit arts organization, also often falls squarely on the ED's shoulders, requiring them to build relationships with donors, write grant proposals, and manage fundraising events. Each of these tasks requires a different skill set and a significant time investment, contributing to an overwhelming workload that can lead to burnout.

Burnout among EDs is a growing concern in the arts sector. The emotional and mental toll of constantly juggling multiple roles can lead to chronic stress, decreased job satisfaction, and ultimately, turnover. When EDs leave their positions due to burnout, the organization often suffers from a loss of institutional knowledge and leadership continuity, making it even more challenging to maintain momentum toward strategic goals.

The Impact of Antiquated Infrastructure on Delegation

A major factor contributing to the ED's overwhelming workload is the inability to delegate effectively. While delegation is a crucial leadership skill, it is often hindered by the structural inefficiencies and outdated processes prevalent in many arts organizations. For example, if an organization relies on manual data entry for financial transactions or uses basic spreadsheets for donor management, it becomes nearly impossible to hand off these tasks without a significant risk of errors or miscommunication.

These inefficiencies create a situation where the ED, who may have the most comprehensive understanding of these convoluted systems, feels compelled to retain control over them. It is not necessarily a matter of mistrusting staff capability, but rather a reflection of the organizational environment where there is little room for error, and the tools available do not support easy or effective delegation. As a result, the ED may default to doing things themselves to ensure they are done correctly, perpetuating a cycle of micromanagement.

Micromanagement, while sometimes perceived as a necessary evil in environments with limited resources, has its own set of detrimental effects. It can erode trust and morale among staff, stifle creativity, and lead to a culture where employees feel disempowered or undervalued. Staff members may become disengaged, as they see their potential contributions minimized or overlooked. This environment makes it difficult for arts organizations to retain talented individuals who could otherwise contribute meaningfully to the organization's mission.

The Vicious Cycle of Overwhelm and Organizational Stagnation

The inability to delegate due to antiquated infrastructure and structural inefficiencies traps EDs in a cycle of day-to-day management, leaving them little time to focus on the strategic leadership that their role ideally requires. As a result, long-term planning, innovation, and organizational growth are sidelined in favor of immediate operational concerns. This lack of focus on strategic initiatives can cause an organization to stagnate, losing its competitive edge and relevance in a rapidly changing arts landscape.

Furthermore, the ED's constant involvement in the minutiae of day-to-day operations can make it difficult to engage in meaningful relationship-building with external stakeholders. Donors, community partners, and board members expect to interact with an ED who is knowledgeable about the organization's broader goals and future direction, not one who is preoccupied with managing minor operational details. The inability to adequately nurture these relationships can lead to missed opportunities for collaboration, funding, and growth.

The Psychological Toll of Role Overload

Beyond the practical challenges, there is a significant psychological toll associated with the ED's conundrum. Role overload, where an individual is expected to fulfill multiple conflicting or excessive roles simultaneously, can result in a range of negative emotional and mental health outcomes. EDs in arts organizations are often deeply passionate about their work, driven by a commitment to the mission and a love for the art form. However, when their days are filled with administrative tasks, and they lack the time or energy to engage with the creative aspects of their role, it can lead to feelings of frustration, inadequacy, and even resentment.

This psychological toll is compounded by the isolation that many EDs experience. As the top executive in the organization, the ED is often expected to have all the answers, maintain a positive demeanor, and be a constant source of inspiration for both staff and stakeholders. Yet, without adequate support and the tools to delegate effectively, the ED may feel increasingly alone in managing the organization's challenges. This isolation can lead to burnout, anxiety, and a sense of being trapped in an unsustainable situation.

The Hidden Costs of the Executive Director Conundrum

The consequences of this conundrum extend beyond the ED's personal well-being to impact the organization in numerous ways. A burned-out or overwhelmed ED may struggle to make sound decisions, resulting in costly mistakes or missed opportunities. They may also lack the bandwidth to engage in strategic planning or to respond effectively to external changes, such as shifts in funding landscapes or audience preferences.

When the ED is bogged down with tasks that should be delegated, it leaves little room for innovation or creative thinking. The organization may miss out on new ideas, partnerships, or funding opportunities that could help it grow and thrive. In the worst-case scenario, the organization becomes increasingly reactive rather than proactive, merely surviving from one crisis to the next without a clear vision for the future.

The Need for Structural Change and Support

Addressing the ED conundrum requires a shift in how arts organizations understand and support leadership roles. One critical step is modernizing infrastructure to enable better delegation and more efficient workflows. By investing in digital tools and platforms that streamline administrative tasks, organizations can free up the ED's time for more strategic work. For example, implementing a robust donor management system can automate many aspects of fundraising, while digital communication tools can improve coordination and collaboration among staff.

Another crucial step is redefining the ED's role to focus more on strategic leadership and less on day-to-day operations. This might involve creating new positions, such as a director of operations or a development manager, who can take on specific responsibilities that currently fall to the ED. By delegating these tasks to capable professionals, the ED can concentrate on guiding the organization's vision, building relationships with key stakeholders, and leading efforts to secure its long-term sustainability.

Finally, arts organizations must recognize the importance of investing in professional development and leadership support for EDs. This could include providing coaching, peer mentoring, and opportunities for EDs to learn from other leaders in the field. By equipping EDs with the skills and resources they need to navigate their complex roles, organizations can foster a healthier, more sustainable leadership model that benefits both the ED and the organization as a whole.

The executive director conundrum highlights a critical challenge facing many arts organizations today: the need to balance operational demands with strategic leadership. Antiquated infrastructure, structural inefficiencies, and an overwhelming range of responsibilities prevent EDs from fulfilling their potential as visionary leaders. By addressing these barriers and providing the necessary support and resources, arts organizations can empower their executive directors to focus on what truly matters: advancing the organization's mission, fostering a vibrant company culture, and ensuring long-term sustainability and impact in the arts community.

CHAPTER 3

STRUCTURAL PROBLEMS AND THEIR IMPACT ON STAFF

When executive directors (EDs) are overburdened and unable to effectively delegate, it creates a cascade of structural problems that affect staff at every level of the organization. These problems manifest in multiple ways, often contributing to a work environment characterized by uncertainty, inefficiency, and low morale. Over time, this situation can erode organizational stability and reduce the overall effectiveness of the arts organization.

Lack of Guidance and Autonomy

One of the immediate consequences of an overburdened ED is the absence of clear guidance and direction for staff, particularly those in middle management or junior positions. In a healthy organizational structure, middle managers play a critical role in translating high-level strategic goals into actionable plans, providing oversight, and fostering communication between upper management and frontline staff. However, when the ED is too overwhelmed to delegate effectively, middle managers may find themselves without the information or authority needed to perform these functions.

This lack of direction often leads to ambiguity regarding roles and responsibilities. Staff members may not know who is responsible for specific tasks or who has the final say in decision-making processes, which can result in duplicated efforts, overlooked responsibilities, and delayed projects. Such confusion can create friction among team members as they struggle to navigate their roles within a disorganized structure, leading to interpersonal conflicts, blame-shifting, and a general breakdown of teamwork.

Disempowerment and Reduced Job Satisfaction

A lack of delegation from the ED also leads to a significant reduction in staff autonomy. When staff members are not entrusted with meaningful tasks or given the authority to make decisions within their areas of expertise, they often feel undervalued and disempowered. This sense of disempowerment can be particularly demoralizing for those in middle management positions who are expected to manage teams or projects without the necessary autonomy or support from senior leadership.

Furthermore, junior staff members may feel that their roles are reduced to mere administrative support or "busywork," with little opportunity to engage in meaningful, mission-driven activities. This lack of engagement can severely impact job satisfaction. Employees may feel disconnected from the organization's goals and disillusioned with their lack of career progression or professional growth. As job satisfaction plummets, turnover rates often rise, leading to the departure of talented and motivated staff members.

High Turnover and Loss of Institutional Knowledge

High turnover rates are a common consequence of the structural problems caused by overburdened EDs. When staff members leave, they take with them valuable institutional knowledge—understanding of the organization's history, processes, relationships, and culture that cannot be easily replaced. This loss of institutional knowledge can be particularly damaging in arts organizations, where much of the work is relationship-based and reliant on long-standing community connections and partnerships.

Replacing experienced staff members also incurs direct and indirect costs, such as recruitment expenses, training time for new hires, and the initial drop in productivity as new employees learn the ropes. In many cases, these new hires are brought in at entry-level positions and may not have the depth of knowledge or experience required to fill the shoes of their predecessors, further exacerbating the organization's existing structural problems.

Compounded by Lack of Investment in Professional Development

The structural problems facing arts organizations are often compounded by a lack of investment in professional development. With limited budgets, many organizations prioritize immediate operational needs over long-term staff development. Unfortunately, professional development is often one of the first areas to be cut during financial constraints, seen as a "luxury" rather than a necessity. However, this shortsighted approach can entrench structural problems and hinder the organization's ability to innovate and grow.

Without opportunities for professional development, staff members cannot develop new skills or bring innovative ideas to the table. This stagnation can lead to a culture of complacency, where staff rely on outdated practices and resist change. As a result, the organization becomes less adaptive and less capable of responding to new challenges or opportunities. Additionally, a lack of professional development opportunities can further diminish job satisfaction and motivation, as staff feel that they have no path for growth or advancement within the organization.

Stagnation and Reduced Organizational Capacity

The absence of clear guidance, empowerment, and professional development ultimately leads to a stagnation of talent within the organization. When staff are not encouraged or equipped to grow, their capacity to contribute to the organization's mission is diminished. The organization may find itself lacking the creative and innovative thinking needed to adapt to new circumstances, respond to community needs, or pursue new opportunities.

Stagnation can reduce the organization's capacity to effectively engage with external stakeholders, such as funders, donors, and community partners. If staff are not able to develop and present innovative programs or articulate a clear, compelling vision for the future, the organization may struggle to secure the financial and community support it needs to thrive. This diminished capacity further perpetuates the cycle of underinvestment in staff development, creating a self-fulfilling prophecy where the organization becomes increasingly less competitive and sustainable over time.

The Importance of Addressing Structural Problems

Addressing these structural problems requires a fundamental shift in how arts organizations view staff management and development. Rather than seeing professional development as an optional expense, it should be considered an essential investment in the organization's future. By providing staff with the tools, training, and autonomy they need to succeed, arts organizations can cultivate a more engaged, motivated, and capable workforce.

Fostering a culture of clear communication, delegation, and empowerment is crucial. Ensuring that EDs are not overburdened and that middle managers have the authority and support they need to lead effectively can help clarify roles and responsibilities, reduce friction, and improve overall organizational efficiency. This, in turn, can enhance job satisfaction, reduce turnover, and preserve valuable institutional knowledge, contributing to a more resilient and sustainable organization.

The structural problems in arts organizations—stemming from overburdened EDs, lack of clear guidance and autonomy for staff, and limited investment in professional development—can have profound negative effects on staff morale, efficiency, and organizational capacity. Addressing these issues requires a commitment to modernizing infrastructure, prioritizing staff development, and fostering a culture of empowerment and accountability. By taking these steps, arts organizations can build a stronger foundation for achieving their mission and ensuring long-term sustainability in a rapidly changing cultural landscape.

CHAPTER 4

THE ROLE OF CULTURAL OPERATIONS SPECIALISTS

In an era where arts organizations are grappling with numerous challenges—from outdated infrastructure and overburdened executive directors to high staff turnover and mission drift—cultural operations specialists have emerged as indispensable agents of change. These professionals bring a unique blend of skills and insights that position them to effectively bridge the gap between an organization's artistic vision and its operational realities, helping to re-align the organization with its mission while modernizing its infrastructure.

Defining the Cultural Operations Specialist

A cultural operations specialist is a multifaceted professional who understands the unique dynamics of arts organizations, which often blend artistic creation, community engagement, financial stewardship, and staff well-being. Unlike traditional management roles that might focus narrowly on specific operational aspects, such as fundraising or marketing, cultural operations specialists approach their work from a broader perspective. They combine a deep understanding of the arts sector with expertise in organizational development, change management, and strategic planning.

These specialists are adept at analyzing an organization's strengths and weaknesses and identifying opportunities for improvement. They possess a comprehensive view of how all parts of an organization—its people, processes, technology, and culture—interconnect and influence one another. This holistic approach enables them to see beyond the symptoms of dysfunction, such as low staff morale or inefficient processes, to address the underlying causes and implement sustainable solutions.

Expertise in Organizational Development and Change Management

Cultural operations specialists are particularly valuable for their expertise in organizational development and change management. They recognize that the resistance to modernization in arts organizations is often deeply rooted in a combination of historical precedent, cultural identity, and resource scarcity. They are skilled in navigating these complexities, understanding that successful change requires more than just the introduction of new technologies or practices; it involves reshaping mindsets, behaviors, and organizational culture.

These specialists utilize a range of tools and strategies to facilitate change. For example, they may conduct organizational audits to identify areas where modernization is most needed, such as outdated administrative processes, ineffective communication systems, or gaps in staff skills and competencies. They may also develop and implement change management plans that prioritize gradual, inclusive transitions, engaging staff at all levels to build buy-in and reduce resistance.

Cultural operations specialists are adept at fostering open communication and collaboration across an organization. They understand that change cannot be imposed from the top down; it must be co-created with input and support from everyone involved. By facilitating conversations, workshops, and training sessions, they help staff at all levels understand the reasons for change, the benefits it will bring, and the role they will play in its implementation. This collaborative approach helps to alleviate fears, build trust, and create a sense of shared purpose and ownership.

Strategic Planning and Mission Alignment

A critical aspect of the cultural operations specialist's role is to help arts organizations develop and implement strategic plans that align with their mission and goals. Many arts organizations struggle with mission drift, where the day-to-day pressures of fundraising, programming, and management cause them to lose sight of their core purpose. Cultural operations specialists help organizations re-center their mission by ensuring that all activities, from fundraising to programming to community outreach, are aligned with the organization's values and strategic objectives.

This strategic planning process often involves revisiting the organization's mission statement, goals, and priorities. Cultural operations specialists work with leadership teams to articulate a clear, compelling vision for the future and identify the specific actions needed to achieve that vision. This might include setting measurable goals, establishing key performance indicators (KPIs), and creating timelines for achieving specific milestones.

By helping organizations develop a focused and actionable strategic plan, cultural operations specialists enable them to make better decisions about resource allocation, programming, and partnerships. They ensure that all efforts are directed toward achieving the organization's mission, rather than being dissipated across a range of disconnected or ad-hoc activities. This alignment not only enhances organizational coherence and effectiveness but also strengthens relationships with stakeholders who are more likely to support an organization with a clear and consistent mission.

Building a Positive and Productive Company Culture

One of the most significant contributions cultural operations specialists make is fostering a positive and productive company culture. They understand that a healthy organizational culture is the foundation for innovation, creativity, and resilience in arts organizations. To build such a culture, they focus on creating an environment where staff feel valued, empowered, and engaged in the organization's mission.

Cultural operations specialists often begin by assessing the existing culture and identifying areas where it may be misaligned with the organization's values or goals. For example, if there is a culture of micromanagement that stifles creativity, they may work with leadership to develop policies and practices that promote autonomy and trust. If there are issues with communication or conflict resolution, they may implement training programs or introduce new tools to improve transparency and collaboration.

Additionally, these specialists are instrumental in developing and implementing programs that support staff well-being and professional growth. They advocate for investment in professional development, recognizing that staff who feel supported and valued are more likely to be engaged and productive. By fostering a culture of continuous learning, they help arts organizations attract and retain talented individuals who are committed to the organization's mission.

Modernizing Infrastructure to Support Organizational Goals

Cultural operations specialists are also key players in efforts to modernize the infrastructure of arts organizations. They bring expertise in digital tools and technologies that can streamline processes, improve communication, and enhance data management. For example, they might recommend the implementation of a customer relationship management (CRM) system to better track donor interactions or the use of project management software to improve collaboration among staff.

However, modernization is not just about technology; it is also about creating systems and processes that support efficiency and alignment with the organization's goals. Cultural operations specialists help organizations identify and eliminate bottlenecks, redundancies, and inefficiencies that drain resources and inhibit growth. They understand that modernizing infrastructure requires a balance between preserving what is valuable from the past and embracing new approaches that can enhance effectiveness and sustainability.

Driving Innovation and Adaptability

In addition to their role in improving internal operations, cultural operations specialists also play a crucial role in driving innovation and adaptability within arts organizations. In a rapidly changing cultural landscape, arts organizations must be agile and responsive to new opportunities and challenges. Cultural operations specialists help organizations cultivate a mindset of experimentation and innovation, encouraging them to take calculated risks and explore new approaches to programming, engagement, and revenue generation.

They do this by fostering a culture that embraces creativity and experimentation. For example, they may support initiatives that encourage staff to develop and test new ideas, or they may work with leadership to create strategic partnerships that bring fresh perspectives and resources into the organization. By promoting a culture of innovation, cultural operations specialists help arts organizations remain vibrant, relevant, and resilient in the face of change.

Navigating Financial Sustainability and Community Engagement

Cultural operations specialists understand that financial sustainability and community engagement are deeply interconnected. An arts organization's ability to attract funding is often directly tied to its relevance and impact within the community it serves. Therefore, cultural operations specialists help organizations strengthen their ties to their communities by aligning their programming and outreach efforts with community needs and interests.

They also bring expertise in diversifying revenue streams and developing sustainable financial models. For example, they may help organizations identify new funding opportunities, such as grants, corporate sponsorships, or earned income through ticket sales, memberships, or merchandise. They might also work with the development team to build stronger relationships with individual donors, ensuring that fundraising efforts are aligned with the organization's mission and values.

The Catalyst for Sustainable Growth

In the face of numerous challenges, cultural operations specialists serve as catalysts for sustainable growth in arts organizations. They bring a unique combination of skills in organizational development, change management, strategic planning, and cultural alignment that enables them to address both the immediate operational needs and the long-term strategic goals of the organization. By fostering a healthy organizational culture, modernizing infrastructure, and driving innovation, they help arts organizations stay mission-focused, financially sustainable, and artistically vibrant.

As arts organizations continue to navigate an increasingly complex and competitive landscape, the role of cultural operations specialists will only become more critical. Their ability to see the bigger picture and integrate diverse elements into a cohesive whole positions them as key players in the ongoing effort to ensure that arts organizations remain resilient, relevant, and impactful in the years to come.

CHAPTER 5

REINVIGORATING COMPANY CULTURE

Reinvigorating company culture is a central task for cultural operations specialists, particularly in arts organizations where the mission extends beyond traditional business objectives to encompass creativity, community engagement, and cultural expression. In these settings, a robust company culture is not merely a backdrop to the organization's activities; it is the very foundation upon which artistic vision, operational effectiveness, and community impact are built. When this culture is neglected or becomes misaligned with the organization's mission, it can lead to a range of challenges, from low staff morale and high turnover to mission drift and diminished public engagement. Thus, one of the most critical roles of a cultural operations specialist is to help organizations rediscover, redefine, and re-embed their cultural identity throughout all aspects of their operations.

Understanding the Importance of Company Culture in Arts Organizations

Company culture is often described as the "invisible hand" that guides the behavior, decision-making, and overall ethos of an organization. It encompasses the shared values, beliefs, norms, and practices that shape how staff, leadership, and stakeholders interact, both internally and with the outside world. In arts organizations, company culture is especially significant because it is intimately tied to the creative process, the way art is produced and shared, and the impact the organization has on its community.

A strong, positive company culture in an arts organization fosters a sense of belonging and shared purpose among staff. It encourages collaboration, innovation, and risk-taking—all essential elements in the creative field. It ensures that the organization remains mission-focused, guiding everything from programming decisions to audience engagement strategies. Conversely, a neglected or misaligned culture can create silos, reduce morale, and undermine the organization's capacity to fulfill its mission.

Rediscovering and Embracing Core Values

Cultural operations specialists begin the process of reinvigorating company culture by working closely with leadership teams to identify or rediscover the core values that should drive the organization. These core values might include creativity, inclusivity, community engagement, artistic excellence, transparency, and sustainability, among others. However, it's not enough to simply articulate these values; they must be deeply understood, embraced, and reflected in the organization's daily operations and strategic decisions.

To facilitate this process, cultural operations specialists often conduct workshops, focus groups, and surveys to gather input from all levels of the organization, from senior leadership to front-line staff. This inclusive approach ensures that the values identified are genuinely representative of the organization's collective vision and are not simply imposed from the top down. Through these conversations, the organization can begin to articulate what these values mean in practice and how they should influence every aspect of its work.

For example, if an organization identifies "community engagement" as a core value, cultural operations specialists might explore how this value can be embedded in everything from marketing strategies (e.g., using inclusive language and imagery) to programming decisions (e.g., offering free or low-cost events that are accessible to all community members) to hiring practices (e.g., recruiting staff and artists who represent the community's diversity).

Integrating Values into Every Aspect of Operations

Once the core values are defined, cultural operations specialists help organizations integrate these values into every aspect of their operations. This is a holistic process that touches on all parts of the organization, from leadership and governance to day-to-day practices and interactions. It involves aligning policies, procedures, and behaviors with the values identified, ensuring that they are consistently reflected in the organization's actions.

For example, in hiring practices, a cultural operations specialist might work with HR to develop job descriptions and interview questions that reflect the organization's values. If inclusivity is a core value, the organization might prioritize hiring a diverse range of candidates and creating an onboarding process that ensures all new hires feel welcomed and supported. Similarly, if transparency is a core value, the specialist might help develop regular communication channels, such as town hall meetings or newsletters, to keep staff informed about organizational decisions and changes.

In program development, cultural operations specialists encourage teams to design initiatives that align with the organization's mission and values. This might involve creating new programs that engage underserved communities, developing partnerships with local artists or organizations that share similar values, or adopting sustainable practices in event production. By embedding the organization's values into its programs and activities, the organization ensures that it remains focused on its mission while also meeting the needs and interests of its stakeholders.

Building a Culture of Trust and Collaboration

A key component of reinvigorating company culture is fostering a culture of trust and collaboration. Trust is the bedrock of a healthy organizational culture; without it, staff members are unlikely to feel empowered to take risks, share new ideas, or fully commit to the organization's mission. Cultural operations specialists work to build trust by promoting open communication, transparency, and mutual respect within the organization. This often involves creating spaces for dialogue where staff members can voice their concerns, share their perspectives, and participate in decision-making processes.

For example, cultural operations specialists might facilitate regular team meetings, feedback sessions, or brainstorming workshops where staff at all levels are encouraged to contribute ideas and provide input on key decisions. By actively involving staff in these conversations, cultural operations specialists help to create a sense of ownership and buy-in, fostering a culture of collaboration and shared responsibility.

Additionally, cultural operations specialists may implement conflict resolution strategies and training programs to address any underlying tensions or conflicts within the organization. By equipping staff with the tools to navigate disagreements constructively, they help to build a culture where differences are respected and collaboration is prioritized over competition or hierarchy.

Promoting Recognition and Celebrating Successes

Another important aspect of reinvigorating company culture is recognizing and celebrating successes, both big and small. When staff feel that their contributions are valued and appreciated, they are more likely to be engaged, motivated, and committed to the organization's mission. Cultural operations specialists play a key role in creating a culture of recognition by developing formal and informal systems for celebrating achievements.

This might involve implementing employee recognition programs, such as "Employee of the Month" awards, or creating opportunities for staff to showcase their work and accomplishments. Additionally, cultural operations specialists encourage leadership to recognize staff contributions publicly, whether through internal newsletters, social media, or staff meetings. By celebrating successes, the organization reinforces its values, boosts morale, and fosters a positive and supportive work environment.

Addressing Cultural Gaps and Challenges

Reinvigorating company culture also involves identifying and addressing any cultural gaps or challenges that may be undermining the organization's effectiveness. Cultural operations specialists are skilled at diagnosing these issues, whether they stem from misaligned leadership, communication breakdowns, or inconsistencies between stated values and actual behaviors. For example, if an organization claims to value inclusivity but consistently overlooks diverse perspectives in decision-making, the specialist will help to highlight these discrepancies and develop strategies to close the gaps.

Addressing these cultural gaps may require difficult conversations and systemic changes. Cultural operations specialists often work with leadership teams to address these challenges head-on, whether by revising policies, reshaping leadership practices, or providing training to staff. They may also facilitate team-building exercises or professional development opportunities that foster a deeper understanding of the organization's values and help staff align their behaviors with these principles.

Measuring Impact and Continuous Improvement

Finally, cultural operations specialists emphasize the importance of measuring the impact of cultural initiatives and continuously improving company culture. Reinvigorating company culture is not a one-time effort; it requires ongoing attention and adaptation. Cultural operations specialists help organizations establish key performance indicators (KPIs) related to culture, such as employee engagement scores, turnover rates, and staff satisfaction levels, to assess the effectiveness of their efforts. They also promote a culture of continuous improvement by encouraging regular feedback and reflection. For instance, they might conduct periodic surveys or focus groups to gauge staff perceptions of the organizational culture and identify areas for improvement.

By fostering a culture of learning and adaptability, cultural operations specialists ensure that the organization remains responsive to changing needs and continuously evolves to better fulfill its mission. Reinvigorating company culture is a vital role for cultural operations specialists, particularly in arts organizations where the alignment of values, mission, and operations is crucial for success. By helping organizations rediscover and embrace their core values, integrating those values into every aspect of their operations, fostering trust and collaboration, recognizing and celebrating successes, addressing cultural gaps, and promoting continuous improvement, cultural operations specialists create a strong foundation for organizational growth and sustainability. Their work ensures that arts organizations remain vibrant, creative, and mission-driven, able to navigate the complexities of the cultural landscape while staying true to their core purpose.

CHAPTER 6

PRACTICAL STRATEGIES FOR MODERNIZING INFRASTRUCTURE

Modernizing infrastructure in arts organizations is a multifaceted endeavor that requires a thoughtful approach. It is not simply about replacing old systems with new ones, but rather about integrating technologies and practices that can better support the organization's mission while preserving its core values and traditions. Cultural operations specialists recognize that modernization must be both inclusive and adaptive, taking into account diverse needs and perspectives within the organization, including those related to neurodiversity and cultural differences. This approach ensures that the transition is smooth, sustainable, and aligned with the organization's goals.

A Phased Approach to Modernization

Cultural operations specialists often advocate for a phased approach to modernization. Rather than attempting to overhaul the entire infrastructure at once, they recommend implementing changes gradually, with careful planning and consideration of the organization's specific context. This incremental approach allows for testing and refinement of new systems, minimizes disruption to daily operations, and provides staff time to adapt to new ways of working.

A phased approach also fosters greater inclusivity by involving staff at all levels in the decision-making process. Input from various departments and roles ensures that the chosen technologies and practices address the actual needs and challenges faced by the organization. This collaborative strategy helps build trust and buy-in among staff, as they see their feedback being valued and integrated into the modernization plan.

Conducting a Thorough Audit of Existing Processes

Before embarking on modernization efforts, a key strategy is to conduct a thorough audit of existing processes and systems. This audit should evaluate the current state of operations, identify inefficiencies, and highlight areas where modernization could have the most significant impact. For example, the audit might reveal that donor records are still kept in paper files, causing delays and errors in fundraising efforts, or that project management relies heavily on email, leading to miscommunication and duplicated efforts.

When conducting this audit, it is essential to consider how different systems and processes affect various members of the organization. This includes understanding how neurodiverse staff members, who may have different cognitive processing styles or sensory sensitivities, interact with existing technologies and workflows. For instance, an employee with ADHD might struggle with a cluttered digital workspace or disorganized project management tools, while someone with dyslexia might find certain fonts or color contrasts challenging to read. By considering these factors, cultural operations specialists can identify specific pain points and areas where new tools could enhance accessibility and usability for everyone.

Similarly, the audit should take cultural differences into account, recognizing that different cultural backgrounds may shape how staff members approach communication, collaboration, and decision-making. For example, in a multicultural organization, some team members may come from cultures where hierarchy and formality are emphasized, while others may prioritize egalitarianism and open dialogue. Understanding these dynamics can help identify opportunities to implement new systems that accommodate diverse communication styles and foster greater inclusion.

Prioritizing Areas for Targeted Investment

Once the audit is complete, cultural operations specialists help organizations prioritize areas for targeted investment. The goal is to make changes that will provide the greatest return on effort and resources while aligning with the organization's mission and values. For example, digitizing donor records and integrating them into a customer relationship management (CRM) system might be prioritized to streamline fundraising efforts and improve donor engagement. Similarly, implementing a digital project management tool could be an initial focus to enhance collaboration, reduce miscommunication, and increase productivity across departments.

Targeted investment might also include tools that enhance accessibility and support neurodiverse staff members. For instance, adopting project management software with customizable interfaces can allow employees to choose layouts and features that best suit their cognitive styles. Tools with text-to-speech options or screen readers can support staff with dyslexia or visual impairments, while color-coding and tagging features can help individuals with ADHD organize tasks and prioritize their work more effectively. In terms of cultural differences, targeted investments could involve adopting multilingual communication tools or platforms that support diverse cultural practices.

For example, an internal communication platform with translation capabilities might be useful for a multicultural team, while video conferencing tools that allow for non-verbal cues and gestures can help bridge communication gaps across cultures.

Investing in Training and Professional Development

A modernized infrastructure is only as effective as the people who use it. Therefore, investing in training and professional development for staff is a crucial strategy for ensuring the success of any modernization effort. Training programs should be designed to equip staff with the skills needed to use new tools and systems confidently and competently.

Training should be tailored to accommodate different learning styles and neurodiverse needs. For example, while some staff may benefit from traditional workshops or webinars, others may find hands-on training sessions or interactive tutorials more engaging and effective. Providing multiple formats—such as written guides, video tutorials, and interactive modules—ensures that all staff can access training in a way that works best for them.

In addition to general training on new tools, specialized sessions might be offered to address the unique needs of neurodiverse staff. For example, training on using screen readers, keyboard shortcuts, or color contrast adjustments can help staff with visual impairments or dyslexia navigate digital platforms more effectively. Training programs should also include awareness sessions to foster understanding and appreciation of neurodiversity and cultural differences within the organization, promoting a culture of inclusion and respect.

Furthermore, training programs can be designed to acknowledge and bridge cultural differences. For example, staff might be trained in cross-cultural communication techniques, such as active listening, non-verbal communication, and conflict resolution strategies that take into account varying cultural norms and practices. This can help create a more inclusive work environment where all staff feel understood and valued.

Creating Inclusive Feedback Mechanisms

A crucial element of modernizing infrastructure is creating inclusive feedback mechanisms that allow staff to express their experiences, challenges, and suggestions regarding new tools and processes. These feedback channels can take many forms, including surveys, focus groups, anonymous suggestion boxes, or regular check-in meetings. The goal is to create a safe space where all voices are heard, especially those from neurodiverse staff or individuals from culturally diverse backgrounds who might otherwise feel marginalized or hesitant to speak up.

Cultural operations specialists can help design feedback mechanisms that are accessible and comfortable for everyone. For instance, some staff may prefer written feedback, while others may feel more comfortable providing feedback verbally. Similarly, in culturally diverse teams, it is essential to ensure that feedback sessions are structured in ways that account for different cultural norms around communication and hierarchy. For example, in some cultures, direct criticism may be considered impolite, while in others, open and frank discussion is valued. Understanding these nuances can help create feedback processes that are more inclusive and effective.

Leveraging Technology for Accessibility and Inclusivity

Modernizing infrastructure involves leveraging technology to create a more accessible and inclusive environment. This includes adopting digital tools that accommodate different neurodiverse needs and cultural preferences, as well as ensuring that new technologies are user-friendly and accessible to all staff members. For example, digital tools with customizable interfaces, voice command features, and compatibility with assistive technologies can greatly enhance accessibility for neurodiverse staff. Project management tools that allow for visual timelines, color-coded tasks, and adjustable notifications can help employees with different cognitive styles manage their workload more effectively.

From a cultural perspective, technology can also be leveraged to bridge cultural divides. For instance, platforms that support multiple languages can help non-native speakers feel more included and ensure clear communication across the team. Video conferencing tools with real-time translation or subtitles can facilitate more inclusive meetings, especially in multicultural teams.

Building a Culture of Continuous Improvement

Finally, a critical strategy for modernizing infrastructure is building a culture of continuous improvement. This means viewing modernization not as a one-time project but as an ongoing process that adapts to changing needs and circumstances. Cultural operations specialists encourage organizations to regularly review their systems and processes, soliciting feedback from staff and stakeholders to identify areas for further improvement. This iterative approach allows the organization to stay responsive to evolving needs and to make incremental adjustments that enhance efficiency, inclusivity, and alignment with the mission.

Building a culture of continuous improvement also involves fostering an environment where experimentation and innovation are encouraged. Staff should feel empowered to suggest new ideas, test new tools, and share their insights on what works and what doesn't. This openness to experimentation ensures that the organization remains dynamic and adaptable, ready to embrace new technologies and practices that support its mission and values.

Modernizing infrastructure in arts organizations is a complex process that requires careful planning, inclusivity, and a deep understanding of the organization's unique needs. By taking into account neurodiversity and cultural differences, cultural operations specialists ensure that modernization efforts are not only effective but also equitable and supportive of all staff members. Through a phased approach, targeted investments, inclusive training, feedback mechanisms, and a culture of continuous improvement, arts organizations can build a modern, efficient infrastructure that supports their mission and enhances their capacity to thrive in a rapidly changing world.

CHAPTER 7

THE BENEFITS OF A MODERNIZED AND CULTURALLY ALIGNED ORGANIZATION

When arts organizations embrace both modernization and cultural alignment, they lay the groundwork for sustained success and growth in an increasingly competitive and dynamic environment. Modernizing infrastructure enables organizations to operate more efficiently, while cultural alignment ensures that these efficiencies are achieved in ways that remain true to their core values and mission. Together, these strategies create a synergistic effect that positions arts organizations to thrive both artistically and operationally.

Greater Efficiency and Resource Optimization

A modernized infrastructure allows arts organizations to achieve greater efficiency by streamlining processes, reducing redundancy, and minimizing errors. For example, digitizing administrative tasks like donor management, ticketing, and financial reporting can free up significant time and resources, allowing staff to focus on higher-value activities that directly support the organization's mission, such as curating exhibitions, developing educational programs, or engaging with the community. Automated systems and digital tools also facilitate better data management and analysis, enabling organizations to make more informed decisions, monitor their impact, and strategically plan for the future.

By optimizing resources in this way, arts organizations can reduce costs, improve their financial sustainability, and increase their capacity to deliver meaningful artistic and community-oriented initiatives. This enhanced efficiency also helps organizations remain competitive in a rapidly evolving cultural landscape, where audiences increasingly expect seamless digital interactions and responsive programming.

Strengthening Company Culture and Enhancing Employee Engagement

Modernization efforts that are aligned with an organization's cultural values help foster a healthier and more supportive company culture. A strong company culture is characterized by shared values, trust, open communication, and a commitment to the organization's mission. When modernization is carried out in a way that respects and reinforces these cultural elements, it can significantly enhance employee engagement and job satisfaction.

A culturally aligned organization ensures that staff feel valued and included in decision- making processes, fostering a sense of purpose and belonging. Employees are more likely to feel motivated, committed, and empowered to contribute their best work when they see their organization investing in tools and practices that enable them to perform their roles more effectively and support their professional growth. This can lead to lower turnover rates, reducing the costs associated with recruitment and training while retaining valuable institutional knowledge.

A cohesive and motivated team is also more resilient in the face of challenges, better able to innovate and adapt, and more likely to collaborate effectively across departments. This sense of unity and shared purpose helps the organization remain agile and responsive to changes in the cultural sector, whether it be shifts in audience preferences, funding landscapes, or broader social trends.

Enhancing Artistic and Community Impact

By aligning modernization efforts with the organization's mission, arts organizations can more effectively leverage their resources to enhance their artistic and community impact. A modernized infrastructure can support more ambitious and innovative programming, expand outreach efforts, and foster deeper engagement with diverse audiences. For example, adopting digital engagement tools allows organizations to reach wider and more diverse audiences, both locally and globally, breaking down geographic and cultural barriers.

A culturally aligned approach to modernization ensures that these efforts remain true to the organization's values and mission. It helps prevent mission drift by making sure that all activities, from digital marketing to donor engagement, are designed to advance the organization's core goals. This alignment not only strengthens the organization's impact but also enhances its reputation and credibility within the community, attracting new supporters, partners, and collaborators.

Building Resilience in an Ever-Changing Landscape

The cultural sector is constantly evolving, shaped by economic fluctuations, technological advancements, and shifting societal values. Organizations that fail to adapt risk becoming obsolete, losing relevance, and struggling to secure funding and audience engagement. Embracing modernization, while maintaining cultural alignment, equips arts organizations with the tools and flexibility needed to navigate these uncertainties.

Cultural operations specialists play a critical role in fostering this resilience by helping organizations strike a balance between honoring their traditions and embracing change. They provide expertise in organizational development, guiding organizations through the complexities of change management and ensuring that modernization efforts are strategically planned and effectively implemented. They act as champions for both innovation and mission alignment, helping organizations remain vibrant, relevant, and impactful in an ever-changing cultural landscape.

Supporting Leadership and Improving Decision-Making

Modernization and cultural alignment also empower executive directors and other leaders to perform their roles more effectively. When infrastructure is modernized, leaders are less burdened by administrative inefficiencies and can delegate tasks more easily, freeing them to focus on strategic planning, relationship building, and artistic visioning. With the right tools and systems in place, leaders can make better-informed decisions based on real-time data and analytics, enhancing their ability to respond quickly to new opportunities or challenges.

When leaders are supported by a positive company culture and a well-functioning infrastructure, they are better positioned to inspire and guide their teams. They can communicate more clearly, articulate a compelling vision for the future, and foster a sense of shared purpose and commitment across the organization. This improved leadership capacity ultimately contributes to greater organizational stability, coherence, and impact.

Fostering Inclusivity and Accessibility

A modernized and culturally aligned organization is also better equipped to foster inclusivity and accessibility, both within the organization and in its interactions with the broader community. Modern infrastructure, including digital tools and platforms, can enhance accessibility for diverse staff and audiences, ensuring that everyone can participate fully in the organization's activities. For example, accessible websites, online ticketing platforms, and virtual event capabilities can make it easier for individuals with disabilities or those who live far from the organization's physical location to engage with its offerings.

A commitment to cultural alignment means that organizations are mindful of the diverse needs and preferences of their staff, audiences, and community partners. By taking into account neurodiversity and cultural differences, organizations can create more inclusive environments that respect and celebrate diversity. This not only strengthens internal team dynamics but also enhances the organization's ability to connect with a broader range of communities, fostering a more vibrant and engaged cultural ecosystem.

Attracting and Retaining Talent and Support

Organizations that successfully modernize while staying true to their mission and values are more attractive to both talent and supporters. A modernized infrastructure that promotes efficiency and innovation, combined with a strong company culture that emphasizes inclusion, respect, and purpose, appeals to prospective employees who are looking for a dynamic and meaningful work environment. These factors also resonate with donors, funders, and community partners who want to invest in organizations that demonstrate both operational excellence and a deep commitment to their mission.

By creating an environment where staff feel valued, engaged, and supported, arts organizations can attract and retain top talent, build stronger relationships with supporters, and secure the resources they need to continue their work. This, in turn, supports the organization's long-term sustainability and impact. The benefits of a modernized and culturally aligned organization are manifold. By embracing change while staying true to their core values, arts organizations can enhance their efficiency, strengthen their company culture, and expand their artistic and community impact. Cultural operations specialists play a crucial role in guiding these organizations through the complexities of modernization, ensuring that every step taken is aligned with the organization's mission and values.

Ultimately, the future of arts organizations depends on their ability to adapt to an ever-changing cultural landscape while preserving what makes them unique. By investing in both infrastructure modernization and cultural alignment, arts organizations can navigate these complexities with confidence, resilience, and purpose, continuing to make meaningful contributions to the cultural landscape for years to come.

ABOUT THE AUTHOR

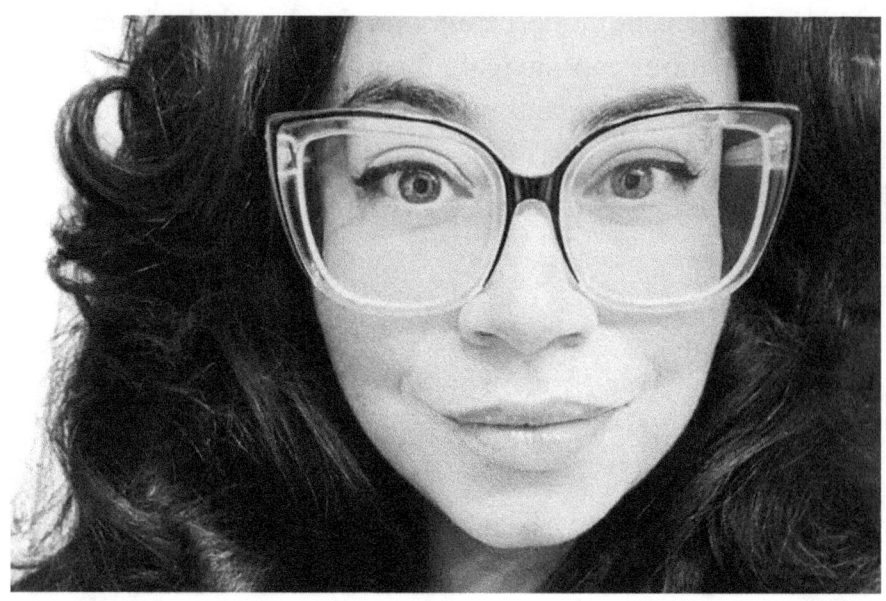

Denise Zubizarreta is a neurodivergent mixed media interdisciplinary artist and Cultural Operations Specialist of Puerto Rican and Cuban descent, with decades of experience in various creative fields. She is currently an arts and culture writer for multiple leading publications that offer curated and critical perspectives on contemporary art, film, television, and culture.

Zubizarreta holds a B.F.A. in Fine Art from Rocky Mountain College of Art + Design, and is completing her Master's in Arts Leadership and Cultural Management (M.A.L.C.M.) at Colorado State University. Her passion for arts and culture drives her to explore and challenge the intersections of post-colonial theory, identity, technology and traditions in her writing and mixed media works.

www.ingramcontent.com/pod-product-compliance
Lightning Source LLC
Chambersburg PA
CBHW070417230526
45471CB00006B/2846